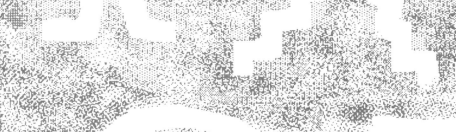
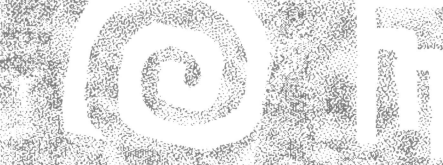

The Love
That Ended
Yesterday in Texas

The Love
That Ended
Yesterday in Texas

Poems by
Cathy Smith Bowers

Texas Tech University Press

for Dennis
and
for my mother
and
in odd, loving memory of my father

Copyright 1992 Texas Tech University Press

This book was set in 11 on 14 Garamond and printed on acid-free paper that meets the guidelines for permanence and durability of the Committee on Production Guidelines for Book Longevity of the Council on Library Resources.

Jacket and book design by Joanna Hill.

Manufactured in the United States of America

Library of Congress Cataloging-in-Publication Data

Smith Bowers, Cathy, 1949-
     The love that ended yesterday in Texas / Cathy Smith Bowers.
       p. cm.
     ISBN 0-89672-301-1.
     I. Title.
     PS3569.M5398L68 1992
     811'.54—dc20   91-19320
                                             CIP

92 93 94 95 96 97 98 99 / 9 8 7 6 5 4 3 2 1

Texas Tech University Press
Lubbock, Texas 79409-1037 USA

Acknowledgments

I would like to thank the General Electric Foundation and the South Carolina Arts Commission for Awards and Grants that bought me time to complete this book. Many of the poems in this collection have appeared in the following publications. Thanks to all the editors for their faith in my work.

The Davidson Miscellany: "The Girl Who Drove the Nail"

The Devil's Millhopper: "Birthright" and "Setting Things Straight"

The Georgia Review: "Aphasia," "Fall," "The Fat Lady Travels," "Hanging the Screens," "The Love," "Namesake," and "October"

Hiram Poetry Review: "Stars"

Iris: "Falling in Love with Sickness"

The Journal: "Mating Season on Firethorn Pond"

The Kenyon Review: "Men"

Pembroke Magazine: "To My Nephew, Age 11 , of His Estranged Father"

South Carolina Review: "Markings"

Southern Humanities Review: "Turning the Myth Around"

Southern Poetry Review: "After Reading It Is Only a Myth That a Person Looking up from the Bottom of a Well in the Middle of the Day Can See Stars," "Bone," "Elegy for My Brother," "One Hundred and Ten Degrees," "Paleolithic," "Third Child," "Saviours," and "Wanting Them Back"

The Wilmington Review: "The Flower We Could Not Name"

Poet Lore: "Thunder," and "To a Friend with a Hyphenated Name, After Her Divorce"

New England Review/ Bread Loaf Quarterly: "The Compass" and "Third Floor West"

Subtract us into nakedness and night
   again, and you shall see begin in Crete
   four thousand years ago the love
   that ended yesterday in Texas.

Thomas Wolfe
Look Homeward Angel

Preface

What drew me to Cathy Smith Bowers' poems in journals was the delight of similes and sounds and exciting closure. I wondered if she could sustain such interest. Reading these collected poems, I began to feel the cumulative power of recurring images and themes which increased both feeling and meaning, the secret of all strong books.

I finished the manuscript's last lines and marveled that we could be so lucky. How could this wonderful book still be available? The editor Judith Keeling and I agreed years ago on one absolute standard for any book that I recommend: "Must we publish this book?" After many readings of *The Love That Ended Yesterday in Texas,* I told Judith, "Yes. Yes."

All year, I had read with excitement poems by hundreds of poets for our first-book series. What a wonderful time to be alive, I kept thinking, amazed at such plenty. When the finalist manuscripts arrived, I found some of the best poems I had read in years. Hard work, lovely, involving many regrets, having to choose from among such gifts.

Cathy Smith Bowers' book was abundant reward for hours of labor, reading all year, giving up time I could have spent with friends and family. For her poems are surprising, even thrilling. Some aspects she has mastered are her sense of closure, similes, and sounds: for example, the closure of "Wanting Them Back," "The Birthmark," "Fire," "The Boxers," and "Thunder"; the tight, imagistic lines and exciting combinations of similes and sounds in "Wanting Them Back," "Stars," "Time," "October," "The Shelter," "Namesake," and "Mating Season on Firethorn Pond."

I also like the wit and playfulness, the inventive twists she gives to serious, familiar topics, as in "Wanting Them Back," "October," "Bone," "Salt," "To a Friend with a Hyphenated Name, After Her Divorce," and "Hanging the Screens."

The first poem of hers I found in a journal was "Wanting Them Back." So much of what I read a poem for is here: the stimulation of specifics and sounds; the convincing turn inward, toward where we live; and a closure that explodes with emotions and discovery—in all, a music richer than I thought mere words would hold.

I remember the excitement I felt on finding this new way of saying one of the most familiar longings since the first bite of the apple. Gone, she writes, are the September cicadas and beetles,

> Even the hummingbirds
> buzzing like neon thumbs
> around the bulbs of sweetened water
> we had hung from the gutter ledge.
> *Good riddance* we said
> when they left for Mexico.

Now, in December,

> One morning we find ourselves at the window,
> staring up at sky's vacant lot,
> wanting them back.
> Like childhoods we wept to grow out of.
>
> Like the man who looked on
> as the boy he had carved from pine
> turned suddenly flesh,
> his painted-on hair bristling to life
> as he leapt to the floor running,
> astonished at the ruckus in his chest,
> at the strange old man at his back
> who kept crying *Be Wood! Be Wood!*

The poem needs to be read whole, of course, and in context; for like all good poems, it is a seamless robe. Oh, I have no doubt the seams could be seen in early drafts—but what cunning needlework, what convincing scissors.

In this wonderful poem are most of the regions she prowls: an exciting natural world which passes; the human heart longing for something it values, most often that which is gone forever; and transformation, discovery of that puzzling ruckus of the vulnerable human heart.

Here is a poetry of terrible beauty which, taken together, makes peace with past demons—not with a sigh or flaccid acceptance, but fiercely, with no easy forgiveness, forged after long hammering in the heart's darkest fires—that struggle we call love. She loves what matters, and like all of us, I suspect, often loves it most after it's gone. Her book doesn't end there, though; it is more than just another cry of ubi sunt.

All experience leads her into compassion and insight. Cathy Smith Bowers feels passionate about injustice and squalor, even rage, but hers is not a poetry of polemics or easy protest. She is too much involved in the fellowship of human toil and longing to hurl easy invectives, too human to draw a line in the dust between *them* and *us.*

She never poses as a saint holier than most of us. Witness the fierce imagery at the end of "The Party" after this early self-mocking irony: "Anyway, for some reason / that was the year I became magnanimous." Rage does not warp her into a Sherwood Anderson grotesque, never jells into monomania repeating how cruel the world, how lonely. Like the thrust of Roethke's best spirit, she learns by going, and bears burdens boldly with hope as in Levertov's "Stepping Westward."

Of all of the father poems I have read, hers are the most convincingly ambivalent. She shares the dark side of a father, starkly, but probes more than only the hateful. She knows what enormous rage love tumbles us into, what radical forgiveness it demands, for better or worse.

In one of those poems, "Fire," she remembers, "once my father set fire / to the closet where my sisters and I kept our clothes." When her mother "smelled smoke coming from the room / where we slept," the mother ran enraged and found her father "in the closet / curled on his hands and knees," beating out the fire he had set "For the insurance money."

> We were in bed asleep and she wanted to kill him.
> To pummel the mouth and nose the way she had found him
> hunkered, slapping at his pathetic flame.

> But all she did was take him to her breast
> and hold him, shaking her head,
> saying Edward, Edward.

The sequence of father poems closes with "The Boxers," about the stained boxer shorts of her father, after he died, estranged from his family, alone. Shocked, she discovers that her sister has not donated them to the Salvation Army with the rest of his old clothes, that paltry legacy, but unaccountably is wearing them, the boxers "whiter, softer now, washed clean." She can't say why her sister has kept them, "Nor why / I took so long to open that package, both wanting / and fearing whatever lay inside."

As much as words can say, though, she shows us the cause of the daughters' ambivalence for their father, their pain and odd longing for such a father:

> Like a child
> huddled by the campfire who cries out in terror
> at the story someone just told
> and, still weeping, begs for it again.

"Fire" and "The Boxers" are fiercely moving; how could anyone not weep? Cathy Smith Bowers' father poems are relentlessly specific, but oh so human, so believable. A poem like "The Boxers" casts us down into the buried life (as Thomas Wolfe, the author she took her book's title from, explored), and lifts us up, as literature can. "The Boxers" lets us feel more human, a poem we can read again and again, with feeling. It is "the human heart in conflict with itself," as Faulkner said, "which alone can make good writing."

Powerful as they are by themselves, "Fire" and "The Boxers" are even more moving read as part of the book, closing that sequence of father poems. They build on the pain and sorrows of the others, and the compassion and sense of loss are more deeply felt. This passionate sequence shows why a good book is more than a random collection of poems.

The simile of that child huddled by a campfire at the end of "The Boxers," for instance, is more than an image to decorate a poem.

x

Appropriate as it is in itself, its impact is even greater in context, recalling an image from "Fire," the preceding poem: when the girls' father set fire to the closet, he "curled on his hands and knees" in that closet "like a lone camper / beating out the campfire's rampant blaze."

This is realistic poetry of joy and love in a world of risk. In the book's last poem, "Hanging the Screens," the image of a wife anchoring her husband as he leans out an upstairs window during a storm gives us a new metaphor for the truism that we are all trying to keep (in Wilbur's words) "a delicate balance" ("Love Calls Us to the Things of This World").

In her sequence of marriage poems, Cathy Smith Bowers shows with wit and clarity what love demands. In "Thunder," a continent away from each other after a month apart, "nursing the anger," the husband in California hears over the telephone the crack of thunder of a Carolina storm,

> And yes, yes
> that is what he misses most
> about South Carolina.

"Not the dust," "Not the lakes of carp and catfish."

> But the way
> when the land is long given up for dead
> and farmers have disinherited the sky
> for good this time
> it breaks sudden and big as forgiveness.

> *They don't have that here,* he says
> as if he were speaking
> of grits or Dixie Beer
> or a woman
> who would stand in a storm
> holding the receiver to the sky.

What joy, someone risking so much for another. "Thunder" is another case of "wanting them back"; but here, joyfully, there *is* another chance to redeem the day. In the book's last poem, so the wife won't have to give up "the thing" she loves most (sitting in her "study during a storm, / the windows up, curtains billowing / like muses above my typewriter"), her husband decides to hang the upstairs screens moments before another storm. With his legs "wrapped tight around [her] waist to anchor him," she imagines what a sight they must be, precarious and exposed in the window in "a position no missionary would take." But if lightning strikes them both,

> What better way to go than this—
> clasped in my husband's thighs high above earth,
> . . . .
> . . . oblivious to the storm.

"Thunder" and "Hanging the Screens" show what people risk to stay together. Lighter, more joyful, they are companion poems which affirm the awful forbearance of love expressed so ambivalently in "Fire."

Young writers are often urged to find the right words, not to be satisfied with early drafts. "After all," we ask them, "how many memorable poems would you have to write to be satisfied? Really memorable poems. One hundred? Fifty? Ten? How many would you hope to have in major anthologies a hundred years from now? Even five?"

Already, Cathy Smith Bowers has finished that many and more which someday editors will have an easy time including, as I did, telephoning friends eagerly to say, "You must read these!"

Walter McDonald
Series Editor

Foreword

The Brain is deeper than the sea—
For—hold them—Blue to Blue—
The one the other will absorb—
As Sponges—Buckets—do—
                    Emily Dickinson

A common criticism of American poetry written in the past thirty years has been that it is too caught up with events and emotions of private lives—and, therefore, too little concerned with vital (and often urgent) public matters: political injustice in its Hydra-headed forms, rampant destruction of the earth's biosphere, or the collapse of humanitarian and spiritual values beneath the weight of a seemingly unstoppable growth in our acquisitive greed. I have been often sympathetic with this perspective on our poetry, but in recent years I have been shifting, with more and more conviction, toward a view that is both contrary and complementary. I have come to believe that a crucial failing of American poetry may be that it has not dared to be private *enough,* has not been sufficiently brave, sensitive, or thorough with its delvings into everyday thoughts and actions. Perhaps all of us—poets, readers of poetry, and nonreaders of poetry—would do well to be reminded of a classic cart-and-horse situation: before chlorofluorocarbons and nuclear fission, before Catholicism and Judaism and Confucianism, before democracies, monarchies, and dictatorships, before money and borders . . . there were *people,* individuals whose urges, fears, skills, and imaginations eventually filled the world with objects, concepts, and ideas that had not existed before.

When I need reconvincing that poetry is indeed the vital creation I want and believe it to be on my better days, I turn most often to the prose of Wallace Stevens—any of it—and to William Carlos Williams' brief essay (from *The Autobiography*) entitled "The Practice." Stevens soars and Williams walks, but they arrive finally at the same place—or equivalent places—in the human heart of hearts:

> *There is, in fact, a world of poetry indistinguishable from the*
> *world in which we live, or, I ought to say, no doubt, from the*
> *world in which we shall come to live, since what makes the poet*
> *the potent figure that he is, or was, or ought to be, is that he*
> *creates the world to which we turn incessantly and without*

knowing it and that he gives to life the supreme fictions without
which we are unable to conceive of it.

Wallace Stevens
"The Noble Rider and the Sound of Words"

We begin to see that the underlying meaning of all [that people]
want to tell us and have always failed to communicate is the
poem, the poem which their lives are being lived to realize. No
one will believe it. And it is the actual words, as we hear them
spoken under all circumstances, which contain it. It is actually
there, in the life before us, every minute that we are listening, a
rarest element—not in our imaginations but there, there in fact.

William Carlos Williams
"The Practice"

No world exists unless poetry creates it for us, and this poetry has its source within every person who lives or has lived—what strange and radical assertions, especially from an insurance executive and a physician! (To reiterate, with another passage from Williams's essay: "Under that language to which we have been listening all our lives a new, more profound language, underlying all the dialects, offers itself. It is what they call poetry.")

Cathy Smith Bowers lays upon herself a tremendous task and responsibility when she takes her book's title and epigraph from Thomas Wolfe: All human thoughts and actions, she asserts, are interwoven at an individualized level— and have been, in a very real way, since the beginning of time. Attention must be paid to everyone and everything because, as in the mythologies of the Greeks and others, we can never know when a beggar at our door might be a goddess in disguise.

On some of the pages that follow, a baby is named for the young girl whose brave televised death captured the spirit of a pregnant woman watching the awful story unfold; a broken man pisses on the ground owned by the company that has taken away his livelihood; and brothers surround their father's bed in the last quarter-hour of his life, touching everywhere the body of this angry man who had kept them always at arm's length. Cathy Smith Bowers' poems pull us back toward nakedness and night, creating once more what Marianne Moore called "a place for the genuine." Such places seem to grow ever fewer and smaller. When the opportunity to reach one arises, let us try— every moment—to listen.

Stephen Corey

Contents

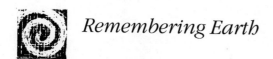 *Remembering Earth*

 *Paleolithic*

We love these old caves—Lascaux,
Altamira—and walk carefully
the way we always enter the past,
our hands bearing
the artificial light of this world.

We imagine those first hunters
crouched, conjuring luck,
carving into rock-swell
their simple art—whole herds of bison,
the haunches, the powerful heads, floating
orderless along the walls.
And some are climbing sky
as if they were stars, planets
orbiting something they cannot see.
Centuries will pass before they
right themselves, their hooves
coming down onto the deep
wet floor of leaf-fall.
Remembering earth.
Remembering where it was
they were headed.

Wanting Them Back

In September we grew sick
of the cicada's impenitent whine,
the beetle's clicking,
raw thorax and bumble of harvestfly.

Even the hummingbirds
buzzing like neon thumbs
around the bulbs of sweetened water
we had hung from the gutter ledge.
Good riddance we said
when they left for Mexico.

Now, as early as December
we are tired of talking to ourselves,
of the body's noisy machinations,
the blood knocking
like a tribe of pygmies beating sticks.

One morning we find ourselves at the window,
staring up at sky's vacant lot,
wanting them back.
Like childhoods we wept to grow out of.

Like the man who looked on
as the boy he had carved from pine
turned suddenly flesh,
his painted-on hair bristling to life
as he leapt to the floor running,
astonished at the ruckus in his chest,
at the strange old man at his back
who kept crying *Be wood! Be wood!*

 *The Party*

Perhaps it was that song those stars
recorded, their arms entwined like ivy,
swaying, their words a joyous proclamation
of brotherhood. Or something some professor
said in class about what it means to be a citizen
of this world. Anyway, for some reason
that was the year I became magnanimous.
The students were throwing a party for some battered
children the department of social services rounded up,
a small herd of defective cattle
we would prod into the season with gifts and song.
The beard the president of the club had strapped
clumsily on jutted from his chin like a shovel
of dirty snow. His red suit, stuffed with clothes
his fraternity no longer wore, preceded him
into the room like the belly of a man
who has given his life to food. He kept ho-ho-ing,
urging the children into the fun, but they hung
at the edge of the room, a neighborhood
they were afraid to step out of. Their hands
and faces had been scrubbed, and still
they looked soiled, their hair the color of titmice,
the washed-out skin, shoulders dangling
like wire hangers beneath their shirts and blouses.
Odd, how, like that bad joke about blacks
and orientals, they all seemed to look alike
huddled there against the wall, as if poverty and pain
like hunched backs were a matter of wrecked
genetics. Odder still, how, when the other games failed

and they were coaxed to the bright pinata, the crepe bull
spinning from the light, they joined furiously in,
went at it with their sticks, fevered,
like a small tribe at the beginning of time
flailing and beating until the soft hide broke
spilling out onto the floor its sweet, dark center.

 *Stars*

There are darknesses here
no one has ever known
like the town
in that strange novel
when the world was so new
things did not yet have names.

Like the room
where my mother's mother
pieced quilts by candlelight
to document her passing.

Tonight, late August,
the month that leaves the skies unseamed,
we spread on a grassy hill
her eight-point star,
so perfect in its symmetry,
each star's bright center holding
as if to verify
such heavens could be tamed.

We expect meteors,
light in all defiance of design,
want stars arcing the sky so wide
our mouths will fill with dust.

You see a bear
and a man who holds

against his ever hopeful breast
that bright bear's death.

I see six sisters
and know the one that's lost
is lost forever.

We lean back into a place
so void of light
it has no name.

Above us sky hangs on its rack,
tattered, threadbare.
That old thing.

 *Time*

The first time I knew
it could not be trusted
I was sick on chocolate rabbits
and a basket of dirty eggs
I had fumbled all morning
on the cemetery's immaculate lawn—
some kind of service for watching the sun rise.

What's Easter? I asked my mother
then stood with my eyes agape
as the words rolled away from her mouth.
Having asked only months before
What's Christmas? it was years
before I could erase from my mind
the horrors I envisioned—a fat, pink
baby Jesus squiggling on a cross.

That fall, a great great aunt
appeared like impetigo out of nowhere
sweet and festering in the heat of dog days.
She moved slow as altar call.
She was old as a railroad tie
across whom the years had clanged and rattled.

As dusk fell and I tumbled in the dewing grass
she rocked on the porch with my mother
and remembered how she, too, deaf

9

to her mother's distant voice,
had made light of dark.

It was only yesterday I heard her cry
as my mother dragged me to bed.
All night I prayed against tomorrow,
against facing at the breakfast table
that rag of skin nailed to those old bones.

 *Birthright*

As early as ten it started.
That fine blue line
on the back of my calf,
that line I thought
my mark of immortality.

Not your voluptuous breasts,
not the heart-shaped lips,
not the plump, soft hands
extended to the world:
Help, here is help for all your needy.

When I was twenty
they told me you were dying.
Half my blood would not
bring you back to life.

Tangle of blue vines.
Mesh of chicken wire.
Bloody wandering jew.
Fish net slung out to dry
on a ragged pier

till year by year
it spread
on the banks of my spindly calf.
A rivulet, a gorge,

bright glacier moving
down the plain of my smooth leg,
my personal cartographer
mapping out the highway of my life.

Mother, look.
Here below the awkward knee
lies the road to Avernus

where you wait
for this body, your proud vessel,
this blood, your Acheron.

Aphasia

My mother whispers *clock, clock*
and points to the old refrigerator
with its hisses and bumps and screeches
we mistook one night for a wild turkey,
fearing all of nature had moved inside.

Every day she drifts farther away,
the disease bearing her backwards
like those schools of salmon
she knew in her girlhood,
their lean and shadowy bodies
leaping the difficult falls.

One by one, names fall away from faces,
each a sloughed-off skin,
a small star burning out. I gather
her words like scattered toys,
jangle them before her eyes,
a ring of bright keys.

I give my mother my daughter's blocks.
Teach her *square* and *round*,
the simple symmetries of childhood.
Then *candle, scissors, watch.*
But for her, each is a flower
that closes in the night.

Like that film old Professor Zaroff
kept showing years ago in botany class—
roses, lilies, azaleas
unfolding before our eyes.
Then, his hysterical laughter
echoing through the corridors,

he began running it backwards
faster and faster, the screen
relinquishing everything
to the whirring reels.

I sat in the dark and watched
as dewy petals quivered, curling
into the slender pistil, into
the whorled womb of calyx
retreating into leaf
into stem and bulb

until nothing was left
but a small mound of earth
and the sun and the moon
chasing each other
across the exhausted skies.

One Hundred and Ten Degrees

Desert moved into town
and made itself at home.
Houses glowed like skulls.
Banisters lined the stoops
like rows of teeth.

Lizards died
and a mongrel dog nobody claimed
whose bones we offered up
like the bodies of virgins.

Our morning prayers
toppled off our tongues
like ancient dances.

Soon, we gave up old religions,
divided what little faith was left
between the sun
who rode her flaming broom
across the sky

and the train,
its empty boxcars
the dark, cool mouths of saviours
luring us inside.

 *October*

No rain for months.
We are dry as when our fathers
swore off booze.
As when our mothers permed our hair
and left us up too long.
We get nervous around matches.

In the shortened days
the trees grow pornographic,
think their time is up,
last chance for love.

They pull on wigs
as red as Orphan Annie's
before her eyeballs failed,
gather faded skirts about their throats,
flash us with what's been too long under—
silk petticoats and panties,
bright contraband imported
by the underworld.

This trick they turn is old.
We are seasoned to it
and do not shock.

The sun, to stave off boredom,
has taken another route,
pulls up in his sequined limousine
and stops.

The leaves
think they have somewhere to go
and start to fall.

16

Turning the Myth Around

*for Dr. George Archibald, who "courted" a whooping
crane to get it to ovulate*

I had hoped for a god
like Leda's.
Huge wings bearing down,
great beak against
the feathers of my throat
transforming me
into the swan
I had always dreamed.

But here's this clumsy mortal
who flails and beats
the air all day
into a thousand shards of light
he must be drowning in.

Still, when the sunlight
falls against his human face,
his eyes ablaze
in the heat of a ritual dance
he has come to love,

something shifts inside me,
begins to move,
like stars thrown out
against the night
where a species of dwindling gods
mourn their own endangered race.

The Birthmark

for my niece

At first we made stories about it.
How in heaven you sold flowers
at the harp maker's gate.
How this one
must have
fluttered
from your hand
clinging
to the moist
new earth of your skin
as you tunnelled
my sister's body
into this life.
Year by year it grew
listing your tiny ankle
like a sorrel bloom.
Changed.
Became iris.
Became violet.
Black mutation of rose.
Soon, it resembled no flower
we could name.
Drifted.
Small island
up the pale wash of your shin,
its beauty darkening
like a song
no man, unbound,
would ever want to hear.

Alzheimer's

All day long
he watches from his window
the small red boat
he thinks is burning.

Its painted flames
flash bright as quills
making history of air.

Every day
the boat comes back
ablaze.

If only he
could get outside,
touch ground,
he's sure his feet
would anchor him to earth,
furrow deep as knotted roots,
the cambium of his heart
ringing another year.

She asks him
what he dreams.
Our children, he whispers,
as she imagines
the sons and daughters
they never had.

Later
on the stairs
she begins softly
to name them.

19

The Love

The love that ended yesterday in Texas
crawled out of the sea
fresh-eared and barnacled,
his lashless eyes astonished
at the shook-out world
where nothing swayed or rippled
but stood one-minded and dry,
pointing forever upward.
He dressed
and boarded a slow boat
that kept him centuries adrift,
finally jumping ship
in a country shaped like a lobster,
the claws of its faraway shores
reaching out to him.
There his journey continued
like the long, slow haul
of a glacier, over mountains,
through gorges and canyons,
across prairies where
ghosts of Indians
whispered his many names.
To the edge of the desert
where he bought a hat
and mounted the horse
that brought him here
to this honky-tonk,
to the corner near the jukebox
where he sits
mourning the woman
whose voice, like the sea,
still calls him.

 *Gravita*

Newton measured
the speed at which an object
falls to earth by rolling it
down an incline, thus slowing
into human proportions
the rate of perpetual motion.
I watched as my teacher
drew in perfect geometric design
the lines and connecting dots,
the little globe stopped
enroute down the dusty board. I don't know
how I passed the test but I understood
well why Newton died a virgin—the small
room they found him in, the pendulums,
the telescopes divesting white light
into its worldly colors.

Years later in Italy
in The Gallery of the Academy,
a young woman beneath the huge, lovely
penis of *David*. She had stumbled, was weeping.
"Gravita! Gravita! " she cried
as she hoisted herself onto an elbow,
her other arm circling her swollen belly
like a moon detached from its planet.

Outside, the olive trees were turning
their silvery spheres toward the light
and somewhere a star, though more
slowly than the apple, was falling.

I Love How My Niece Loves Jesus

I love how my niece loves Jesus,
how the white testament
fits the little fold of her hand
like the purse she sometimes carries
filled with make-believe rouge and mascara.
Or the way a bean seed nestles
in the cupped palms of cotyledons.

And, yes, I love him too, I say when she asks,
imagining what it would be like—his body
falling through mine, hair listing
his shoulders like a biker's,
the good heart and tongue.
And the fall taking centuries
before we are back to where we were
when God that first difficult day cracked
like a paramecium, like an egg,
like a small ship against the rocks
whose prow and stern
now drift
toward separate edges of the world.

 *Old Rain*

Namesake

*for Cathy Fiscus, 3 , who died in an abandoned well
the summer of 1949*

From the face of the earth
is how they put it
when someone disappears
so all day your father paces
among bulldozers and cranes
as your mother sits in the car
muttering to the visor.

I hang in my own mother's womb,
little turtle, zeppelin of skin and marrow.
The chipped ice she craves
grinds in her teeth
like pneumatic saws.

And because television that summer
will be the closest thing to miracle,
she gives in to the sloppy recliner,
to the window fan's rattle and clack
to watch as hour by hour
hope fails in black and white.

Down there you must have heard something queer.
A scraping at earth, some ancient burrowing.

And what word can name the descent of midgets
armed with buckets and spades?

You lived two days, your voice
tamping at the surface, that one song
rising now and then into the suspended mike.

Then—air, light. The blood
hammering at the soft closure
of my skull, they lifted
me out, all slag and sediment,
sludge of another life,
and gave me your name.

Falling In Love with Sickness

After the next one was born
and mother abandoned my bed
to take up with the pink, wrinkled thing,
its eyes stuck shut with mucus,
wispy hair clotted to its head,
the small cave of its mouth
sucking out her life,
I rolled over into the warm grave her body left
and fell in love.

Flu and scarlet fever.
Diphtheria and mumps.
Then willing myself yellow,
I leaned back into the down of quilts and pillows
as jaundice crept over my body.

My limbs racked and shuddered with chills, glowed
with fever's bright hallucinations,
erupted in sores and ulcers,
those rare jewels of dog days
glistening against my skin.

I licked my tongue into the sugar bowl
lapping up the forbidden grains,
the sweet promise of diabetes,
and imagined my mother
easing the daily needle into my skin.

I dreamed of steamy jungles,
malaria riding on the wing and buzz of insects.
Waded in filthy ponds

27

hunting that old frog typhus,
the charmed prince of stagnation
longing for my kiss.

Coughed, wheezed, and vomited
until Mother came back to my bed,
fluffing pillows,
bearing bowls of grapes and oranges,
that warm jar of mentholatum
she rubbed into my chest,
quieting the small animal that rattled there.

One by one she drove them all away,
each walking out of my life
like a friend she did not approve of.
When she went back to her ironing,
to the pots boiling on the stove,
the dirty floors,
to the whimpers and cries of that other one
who had mastered some chronic ailment,

I dragged myself from bed and slowly dressed, pausing
to breathe the last sweet smells
of the sickroom, then turning
stepped quietly through health's lonely door.

Asthma

The walls, like thunder,
threaten to move in closer.

Her mother has rubbed a poultice
into her skin.
Her chest is that heavy fish
her brother pulled
from Bender's Creek in June.
A frying pan.
Fat cat too old to move.

The air is a bubble
that drifts above her mouth,
a rainbow window on each side
like the one you catch again
upon the ring you blew it from
and hold for one last moment.

Mornings
she can see from her high window
children playing
on the banks below,
their laughter like frantic birds
beating against the sill.

They tug and pull
at one another's hands,
at pockets, belts and cuffs

each in his own small need
to drag the other down

to become king of the hill
higher than the trees,
the chimney tops,
higher than the clouds
where she believes
there must be air enough
for even her.

Markings

*Besides the many rituals utilizing various kinds
of markings, a mother might cure an asthmatic child
by marking her height with a green reed.*

These markings on the wall
might mean the nights
a mother counted home her son
or the things she could have said
to make him stay.

First one mark. Then another.
Two more. And now a slash across
them all makes five. And then
five hundred. Until the county
threw the woman out. Left the wall
that marked the history of her grief.

When I was ten my mother
held my back against the northern wall,
the one that shook each time
the train came through.

*Make sure the reed is green,
and from the water's edge*, she'd say—
and the child's back flush to the wall.

*Mark her height precise
and careful as the dress you'd cut
to please the mayor's wife.*

*Make sure it's spring
and when the child has grown
beyond the mark, note
how her breath has eased.*

We women know this art
like a lover's face we might
have traced so lightly as he slept,
marked each feature as if our hands
could memorize the high cheek bones,
firmness of the chin.

We pass it down, this need
to validate the things
we did or did not do,
said or should have said.

Still, there's something in it.
The woman who took up weaving
knows the wall's still there.
I breathe against a pane of glass
and cannot see my breath.
And on nights so long
the moon becomes a man I cannot stand,
I cup my palms and almost see your face.

Men

The summer I was ten
my mother fell in love with Elvis.
I watched her swoon into the TV set
moaning Love Me Tender to the screen,
my father's supper burning on the stove.
One morning she combed
the cotton from her hair,
packed a canvas bag
and took the train to Memphis.
When she came back
I asked where Elvis was
and she cried for days.

Men! I remember her saying years later,
me sixteen and broken-hearted
by a boy across the tracks
whose name I never knew.
Morning until dusk
I walked the brooding rails.
Through June and through July
and into August
until summer loaded up and left
the way a yard sale closes down at dark,
the racks of faded dresses hauled back in.

We both survived.
That boy moved away to Kansas
and the county covered up the tracks
with pitch and tar.
Father took Mother back
and never mentioned Elvis.
And mother never burned his food again
nor sang.

The Girl Who Drove the Nail

August and you're ten again.
In the elbow tree's crook of arm
you sit all day and watch
as air sags
like heavy hives of bees
dreading winter.

And it is the time
when mother left,
her thin frame
rippling with the heat
in that strange way
heat rises
from tracks in summer.

Your eyes see distances
never known before,
grow dim,
retrace to where a turtle
hauls across the ties
something vague
and heavy as a planet.

Through an older wound
the nail drives quick
into the patterned back
deep into design

past heart
through gut
to stone.

He grows into the tracks
like nothing's changed.
Moon lugs night across the sky.
Rivers, whole forests learn.

The Shelter

for my grandfather

Sun, July, could send us scuttling
for the saving hole
you'd dug for us.
October blew dry leaves
across the top like rats
where far below we thought
their scratchings bombs.
You taught us what we needed.
How to add the cans and jars
divided by the number who survived.
Our spelling words were
aerial and *bombardment*
and the two we never could pronounce—
Hiroshima, Nagasaki.

No matter. What bomb
could find us there?
What death, when all along
those muddy walls grew jars
of beans and corn we lifted
to their shelves like porcelain dolls.
The war we waited for refused to come.
Still, you taught us well
the rudiments of breaking ground.
When we climbed out
the sky still looked the same.
The silo held the sun up like a prize.
The spotted cow, who'd watched
as we went down, looked up
indifferent as the clover on her tongue.

Elegy for My Brother

You joked it was devil's shoestring
that you sowed,
not oats,
but poppy, larkspur, clover,
your pollen floating everywhere
to towns so far away they had no names,
to a war where you died
though they sent you back alive,
the brilliant map of your body
the work of skilled cartographers
whose faces you never even saw.

Hot.
It was so hot there,
you awakened one night screaming,
the ice I brought to cool your fever
melting into rivulets
on your brow
until the cold transferred us laughing

to the summer
Mama's Frigidaire blew up
and every morning
you were sent for ice
from the plant across the creek,
that one huge block a day
you dared bring back by way of stepping stone.

I watched from the edge of our back yard
as you emerged from the mouth
of the ice plant

lugging that heavy block
like a sleeping child,

how once on the curved, slick surfaces
you balanced like a circus star
above the creek's shallow death
pretending now and then to lose your footing
until I wept and laughed at the water's edge
then cheered you on to safety.

The fever eased. You slept
and dreamt, as I imagined,
your scattered seed children:
what strange countries' meadows
they frolic through,
the wreaths of poppy, larkspur,
devil's shoestring
circling their delicate heads;

what waters they linger towards
like rats after some faint note
that in another time and place
might have come close to music;

what darkness they tightrope over,
bearing your heart inside them
like ice.

The Compass

When Father finally packed his bag and left
one Sunday after Mother called him a derelict,
I looked up the word in Funk and Wagnalls
and finding that it meant an abandoned ship,
thought how alike we were. Always dreaming
of traveling. Free. Sailing out of that dirty
millyard. Columbus and Vespucci, searching
some secret passage. Lands of spices. Diamonds,
gold and silver. The startled natives
bowing as if we were gods. Next day

in science class, Mr. Hanson gave each of us
a compass to keep, tried to teach us north,
south, east and west. But when he said the compass
always pointed north, my face fell. I glared
at him the rest of the period, wondering
who in his right mind would always want to go
north. An uncle had been there, had warned me
about the place where they mug you in broad
daylight, talk funny, don't understand
real English. I took the compass

home and put it in a drawer beneath the gown
my mother was saving
for when she died. That night I dreamed
of China and Rome, those pink and orange
countries in my geography book, flat paper mountains

my fingers could easily climb, oceans
calm beneath the safe ship of my hand. In the middle

of the night, when I got up to pee, I found my father
slumped, a sunken steamer, across the couch, his suitcase
leaning against the table like a terrible anchor. I

went back to bed, clutching the compass
I had dug from the bottom of the drawer, its smooth glass
sweating in my hand like a flattened globe, and changed
my mind, began planning that slow journey north.

Bone

We became addicted to chaos after years
of living in the midst of trauma.

from a "Laundry List"
for children of alcoholics

Our house was a needle's eye
you shoved a camel through.
You gave us each a bone.
Arm finger toe and ankle
to be tucked in childhood's baggage
and lugged around from day to day
as if always we waited
to board some invisible train.
When you finally died
we were surprised
at the benignancy of doors,
passivity of pots and pans,
the incipient incipience.
The quiet you left
hunkered in corners
like sacks of tongueless kittens.
For a while we kept our distance,
trying hard to love the silence
then one by one
we gathered with our sticks
and began to poke.

Rosie, Old Rain

Suddenly, out of the chronic cyclone
of our parents' arguing
she would spin, tiny dervish
from their center, tapping
and whirling across the linoleum
to the kitchen table
where she would climb
amid the bowls of beans and okra.
And nothing we had seen on *Wild Kingdom*
came close to that hair
spuming out like foam
her elbows and wrists
furious as the hinged skinny legs
of shadow puppets, small shaman
dancing the devils out.
And always Mother, stunned into distraction,
would turn to scold and lift her down
as Father slunk sobering from the room.

Sometimes, hours after lightning, hard wind.
When quiet and the swayed trunks of pines
have righted themselves again
there arises the slightest breeze
and we are called from the debris and broken limbs
to the tops of trees where, listen, somewhere
in the branchy green sphere between sky and earth
there is the dance of old rain raining.

Losses

 *Losses*

Each morning, as sun calls back
from the grass its lent vapors,
that crew of little spirits rising for work,
my retriever begins his ritual of cheeps and chirps
like a nest of sparrows or those biddies
parents buy at Easter for their children
knowing they will die. He won't soil his pen,
so by the time I've had my coffee
and staggered to the yard to let him out,
he is desperate, bolts through the gate
and across the path he has worn in our lawn.
He circles and circles, sniffing out
the perfect spot, lifts his leg, then lopes,
as he was trained, into the woods,
to the sweet mulchy floor of pine and cedar.
Again he sniffs, circles, then curves
his tail-end under like a giant hook or comma.
The Muslim in him faces east
where the scarab sun climbs the sky's moist web.

It doesn't seem right, watching him.
Hunched like an aborted fetus. Straining.
His legs trembling. His soft eyes
averted from my insensitive gaze. The way one summer
in Indonesia, that woman, bathing
beneath the ashy rise of Gunung Agung,
turned shyly away as our cameras continued to click.
She had waded, naked, with her youngest to the bank

where he stooped like a little frog, emptying
his bowels onto the sand. Was it then I knew
I would never have children? Could not bear
at so close a range those leaks
and solvents. Would get instead a dog
I could train to go off into the woods
carrying deep into shadow the body's chronic losses.

Salt

Bane of slugs. Saviour
whiter than the snow and ice
it melts in winter
clearing roads and sidewalks,
swelling gutters to rivers of salty sludge.
Moniker for sailors
who watch from the wharf on Saturdays
or haul, each summer, to the Cuttysark
carloads of grandchildren
dreaming instead of Disney World.
And when my grandfather began
the slow sloughing off into death,
it was the first to go.

In Grandmother's pantry, rows
and rows of jars shattered light
like a rose window. Everything
good—smoked, cured, or pickled.
Quarts of sauerkraut, scarlet medallions of beets.
Peaches, those vinegary sweet yolks
she slithered from a spoon into our mouths.

As we salted the starry centers of apples
Grandmother's bread rose like a soft moon
and she told bible stories

to horrify us into goodness. The snakes,
the floods we had somehow missed, the disobedient
woman turned to salt.

And what did Grandfather mean,
who, in the next room, kept mumbling
not worth his salt, about the migrant
Grandmother had hired to run the farm?

So he ate his last meals bland
and talked of salt
the way an old man remembers lovers
long since gone to rag and toothless.

To a Friend with a Hyphenated Name, After Her Divorce

Because neither name
made commotion enough to matter,
you jammed it there
like a doorstop
between the bed and bath
of love's vacation house
and kept them both.

Stay! Stay! you cried
pointing your finger
and like a good dog
it whimpered once
and lay down.

Now, it is an orphan
left on your backporch step.
It has lost its sweetness.
It has lost its teeth.

It pokes about those empty rooms
like your grandmother's old nose.
Stake without a garden.
Length of firewood that will not burn.

Little amputee,
mutation with no thumb
trailing your name like a proffered hand
no one wants to shake.

When the moon is full
it is your broomstick.
You make your rounds,

an item as they say,
cackling through the night
at your own bad joke.

When dawn brings you home
you lay it down beside you
in the dark.

To My Nephew, Age 11 , of His Estranged Father

At first you will dress him
in beggar's rags
and bring him home.
And after twenty years,
unlike the dog
so old his ragged heart gave out,
you will pit him, bow in hand,
against two hundred warriors.

Or you will find him
one day in history class
stepping down from a flashing cockpit
and off the screen
to walk the projected beam
like a magic runway
into the room,
cradling his battered helmet
like a son

and you, startled into waking,
will not care
what war has brought him here.

Soon, he will be the lineman
you watched in secret
all that August day

as faceless voices snapped
then died among the wires
in his hands.

Or just the taxi driver
eating his peanuts
through the empty streets.

You know where
he would take you
and still
you want to go.

 *The Cure*

for Beth Couvillion
1954-1989

Long after I thought
I had done with grieving
there arose in my chest
between the sternum and clavicle
a soft commotion, like the gerbils
caged in my niece's room
that race all night across the furious wheel.
It would start when I least expected—
in the theater during credits
or among the squash and spinach
of the produce aisle. My breath
would catch, my hand flutter to that spot
the way a mother's hand
rises instinctively to her child's brow
as if touch itself could bring the fever down.

Anxiety attacks, my doctor said,
scribbling in hieroglyphics his perfect cure.
I took the pills, and sure enough
the palpitations stopped, packed up and moved
like a band evicted from the premises.
But I found I missed
that little tuning up of cymbals and drums
the way I still missed you
and threw the pills away.

 *Commute*

The year my father was dying my mother
fell in love. Evenings, after my drive from
the hospital, she would call, who years before
had fled the minefield of our home,
to talk as if we were girls, her voice beating
like wings in the bad connection. And
she would speak of strange clamorings
beneath her skin. Something rising—parturient.
A soft ruckus of spears and drums
as if the little lost tribe of her sex had
stumbled suddenly into sun.
I dreaded that commute between the living and dead
to where my father lay, the impotent
machine humping the fagots of his lungs.

The Watch

Between the time the doctors
switched off the life machine
and you died
I watched how my brothers
in those fifteen minutes
touched every part of your body,
you who had never touched them.
And I saw how they went at you,
grazing the pale lichens of your skin,
the wet mouths of bedsores,
their foreheads tensed
like the brows of small boys
examining their dog for ticks.

And then they were under sheets,
their hands kneading the dumb blue
box of your chest, pocked ankles and shins
the spent penis that shot
the sperm we wriggled out of.
I felt suddenly shy watching like that,
your sons, after all those years,
having their way with you.

Third Floor West

Even after the heart and breath lines
on the screen above my father's head
went straight as the lines down highways
that separate the coming from the going,
one eye refused to close, kept staring
into the room, green and slippery as a beached fish.
My brother kept passing his hand in front of it
the way coroners in old westerns
test the dead for reflex. A film
covered the dark pupil, the iris
pale and swimmy as the yolk of an egg.
At intervals my brother would walk away
to fumble the leaves of the philodendron
some relative had sent, and then return
to ask again where the doctor was,
why he had not come to close it.
Finally a nurse appeared, and to calm my brother
placed her hand flat against my father's brow
and eased her thumb across the lid
like a woman drawing shades in a small house
long after the lights are out.

 *Fire*

After he died, my mother told
how once my father set fire
to the closet where my sisters and I kept our clothes.
It was a day in September, too early
for that odd angle of light that signals fall,
too cool for a Carolina summer, as if
October had seeped from its proper space
in the feed-store calendar behind the stove, bleeding
through to the page above, to the quiet
bowed heads of September's elk and bison.

We were thumping doodlebugs
across the cool, damp earth beneath the porch
and she was in the kitchen kneading bread
when she smelled smoke coming from the room
where we slept. She ran with the sticky milk
and flour oozing between her fingers. She ran
like a woman flaming, mad through the burning doors
of an asylum some psycho set fire to.
And there he was, my father, in the closet
curled on his hands and knees like a lone camper
beating out the campfire's rampant blaze.

For the insurance money, he told her later
when she asked why he had done it.
He wouldn't have let it hurt us, he said,
or the rest of the house,

just a few old clothes we could no longer wear.
We were in bed asleep and she wanted to kill him.
To pummel the mouth and nose the way she had found him
hunkered, slapping at his pathetic flame.
But all she did was take him to her breast
and hold him, shaking her head,
saying Edward, Edward.

The Boxers

When my father, after twenty years, came home
to die, circling, circling, like an animal
we believed extinct, it was my crazy aunt
who took him in, who told later
how the taxi had dumped him
bleached and whimpering on her porch.
And she who had not lived with him
thought his sons and daughters cruel
not to come when he began to call our names.

He died, and soon after, a package in brown wrapping
arrived at my address. My sister, who did not
attend the funeral, kept urging me to open it
and I kept saying I would, soon. Every day
when I came home from work, there it was
sitting at my back door, the remnants
of my father's life—years in the mill
spinning and doffing, then drinking into morning
as he railed at the walls, the cotton
still clinging to his fists. Weeks had passed

when finally my sister and I, after two stiff bourbons,
began to rip the paper, slowly in strips
like archaeologists unclothing a mummy.
And all that was there were a few plaid flannels,
the jacket to a leisure suit, and a pair of boxers,

white and baggy, Rorschached in urine—a smaller
size, my sister said, than the way she remembered him.
Then she offered to drop the things at the Salvation Army
store she passed on her way home. In July

we went shopping for swim suits and I could
see her in the curtained stall across from mine.
She was pulling her slip over her head when I saw
she was wearing them, her thighs like the pale stems
of mushrooms emerging from the boxers' billowy
legs, whiter, softer now, washed clean. I still

can't say why my sister, that day in the Salvation
Army store, glanced up, as I've imagined,
to see if anyone was watching

before she slipped those boxers from the soiled heap
of our father's clothes. Nor why
I took so long to open that package, both wanting
and fearing whatever lay inside. Like a child
huddled by the campfire who cries out in terror
at the story someone just told
and, still weeping, begs for it again.

 *Thunder*

 *Fall*

On a day when the world has just begun
to pack it all in,
the earth luxuriant with decay,
mushrooms littering the ground
like golfballs
some boy has resurrected for money,
I catch sight of my husband
from the upstairs window
where I am hanging curtains.

His broad back is turned to me
where he stands at the edge of the garden
and although he is not a religious man
he holds his hands in front of him
clasped low like someone praying.
His face tilts toward the sky,
toward the baring ash and maple,
the dogwoods clotted with autumn berries.
His head turns slowly from side to side
and I imagine his eyes are closed
as in the last unearthly moments of love.
Then I see that he is pissing.

Squirrels and chipmunks scatter.
A flock of starlings has risen
to the highest limbs of the sweetgum
and the dog retreats
to the safety of the woodpile

as the torrent spatters
onto shriveled bean vines,
parched okra, the shrunken heads
of cabbage. And in the room above

I am thinking, This is what it's like
to be a man caught between luck and ruin.
Like my father the night the mill shut down.
How I found him there in the coalyard
where long chutes disappeared into the spinning room,
the cotton clinging like angel hair
to his Adam's apple.
As starlight rode the beautiful arc of his urine
onto the gleaming coalpile
I stood in the shadow of the smokestack
watching him do
the very worst a good man can do,
the curses catching in his throat
like bad machinery:
piss on it piss on it piss on it.

The Fat Lady Travels

On any train
she is the occupant
of either seat.
No hopes for a handsome stranger.
No petty arguments
as to who
will get the window
or the aisle.
She gets them both.

When she dreams
she is never the goddess
turning men to pigs.
She is the pig.
She is the one gross eye
of the Cyclops
fending off the spears
of her disgrace.

She is all of Brobdingnag.

Her green dress blowzes
in the halcyon wind.
She is turgid water
flooding the station,
home for leviathans.

What she should lose
would be enough

to make the sister
she never had.

And how thin
the both of them would be
gliding on fine-point skates
across some fragile pond

and, oh, it holding!

Setting Things Straight

*Actual insanity is apt to be shown in a sharp change
in the habitual way of writing. The slovenly writer
becomes neat and precise and the careful writer
begins to be almost totally illegible.*

Mumford's *Graphology*

Her eyes migrate, she thinks,
like the ugly fish
that always, eyes-side up,
mistakes the sky for home.

She thinks the minutes months.
Morning, June, she walks
a garden path toward late November
where the carcass of a scarecrow sleeps.
The ground she'd hoped
to gather supper from
lies hard and fallow.

Empty basket heavy as the moon,
she turns in fear that home again
an April scent of green
could mangle her.

She wants the planets
all in place once more,
the moon and stars aligned.

One day in early spring,
the morning long,

she tries to imitate
her girlhood alphabet

each *o* precise and round
as the angel's mouth
that lolled for months
above the tinsel and the lights
then toppled from its brittle height
to where,
like snakeskins,
ribbons curl beneath a tree
that should by now have been
first flame, then smoke, air,
and memory.

Third Child

*There is no such thing as a dyad, only remnants of an
excluded third.*

Carl Whitaker

You have to believe it would have been the one
to save you all. The miscarriage. The abortion.
Or the night between the mill's last whistle
and your mother's freshly powdered skin,
your father chose instead to count stars all night
as if counting, like a poultice
against the sky's dark wound,
would draw them down.

Your mother went to sleep
mad as a moon-ridden woman, her womb
shutting down like the mill when times
were hard, your father laid off again.

It might have been a sister.
One who would have let you wear her clothes.
Crinolines. Pearl-studded collars.
You would have learned together
what to do with hair, the secrets
of eye shadow, bright lipsticks.
And when the blood began its journey down your legs,
you would have knelt together
in the locked toilet, arms about each other
warding off the death it must have meant.

Or a second brother.
A good one this time.
Face too soft for battering.
Heart so sweet it would have gathered

the broken family in
the way street people, wintering,
migrate from under bridges,
from out of bags and boxes
to huddle about a flaming bin.

Saviours

My father had one saviour, booze.
And though I hated the old breath
rank as that rabid hound
he cornered one afternoon
in the blinding forsythia,
the shot ringing out
as we watched the crazed thing
leap once into the air
and then touch down
spinning like a small tornado
in the red Carolina dust,
I had to admire his consistency.

It was you, Mother, I couldn't forgive
after you walked out on Jesus
then flitted for years like a lost angel
from one saviour to another.

How you wept all one summer
for Michelangelo,
each morning at breakfast
planning the pilgrimage
you would one day take
to that chapel where his spirit
still floated, you said,
in the steep dome
for lack of a better place.

I pretended to listen
as I ate my oatmeal
and thought of Nancy Owens.
Once on the schoolyard swing

I watched her long legs
shove backwards against the dirt
then swing forward, pushing out and up
higher and higher
until she was touching the sky,
her toes pointing toward heaven

where she hovered for a moment
then, the long chains looping the bar,
came down in a swell of dust.

The winter you went back
to Jesus, an estranged wife
lugging your heavy suitcases,
I thought of that day
Nancy Owens left earth
and then, before my eyes,
came back alive,
the long smooth arc of her body
dark against the sky,
something I had seen and could believe in.

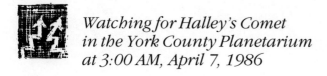

Watching for Halley's Comet
in the York County Planetarium
at 3:00 AM, April 7, 1986

Like that date I knew in high school
it doesn't show.
Like Jesus, after the long
shadowy drowning when I was twelve,
my face crushed
beneath the preacher's hand
that finally after years
dragged me flailing and coughing
to the river's edge, to the towel
that hung like a saviour
across my mother's arm.

The sky still empty twenty years later,
we sit beneath the domed ceiling of the planetarium
bright with artificial stars, as the amateur
astronomer points with his luminated stick
to the spot where it would be
if the clouds miraculously parted
and the comet blazed across the heavens
like the children of Israel.

He dances embarrassed
across the dome of our disappointment,
lids of our groggy eyes as we drift
in and out of sleep, catching his random words:

Scorpius and *Mars. Taurus* and *Perihelion.*
Then in his trembling voice
something about last night,
how right off 77 from the window
of his truck, it bloodied the entire sky.

And again I am a schoolgirl
trying hard to believe
what the eye cannot see.
Like years ago, tenth grade,

my end-of-semester science report,
how from memory, that vague
affair of the heart I had learned to count on,
I rattled off before the entire class
everything there was
not to know about Venus.
How there the lightning flashes
and thunder rolls incessantly,
the atmosphere so thick
a person might swim right through.

I pointed with a long stick
at a chart my teacher
had suddenly pulled from nowhere,
an attic of visual aids
filled with documented sightings,
foil comets,
bright charts of constellations.

Some secret place in the ceiling
where dates could be pulled
like rabbits out of hats
74

and men coaxed from the dead
at a moment's notice,
amazing the eye,
staving off the heart's suspicions
for a little while.

After Reading It Is Only a Myth That a Person Looking up from the Bottom of a Well in the Middle of the Day Can See Stars

I say, whoever decided that has never been there.
Listen. I was a schoolgirl just trying
to avoid recess's lonely corridors
where I had stood four days in a row
amidst an orgy of lockers
watching Susan Jones and Tommy Hough
feel each other up.

So, on Friday when the bell rang,
feigning an odd obsession for logarithms,
I talked Miss Hodgins into leaving me alone
in that dusty room filled with algebra books, tools
of perfect calculation,
the long skinny legs of compasses rigid and spread
that somehow made me need for once in my life
a schoolroom any color but green.

I jammed a stick of red chalk
into the hinged leg of Miss Hodgin's giant compass
and in minutes marked up the room
with hundreds of red circles,
their bright arcs overlapping like arms and legs
across tops of desks, across blackboards
filled with immaculate equations, across
floor and walls until the room was a bloody web

and me hanging out the window screaming, my head
and torso wedged in the slanted pane.

That's how I got there.
Down. Flip-flopping over the rim
like a too-small fish thrown back into the water.
For months I hung just below the surface,

staring up at the curious faces who came and went.
Vague groups of two and three.
Miss Hodgins. Susan Jones and Tommy Hough.
And always some stranger in white.

All reaching down.
Their mouths remorseful and agape,
the whites of their far-away eyes
arranging themselves above
like constellations.

The Flower We Could Not Name

Clematis climbs the weathered
rail we split, and seizes
all within its grasp—green
tendrils, small antennae, tenacious toed
and fingered. Clinging.
Like the boy they pulled
from the reservoir, his arms
and legs in the muscle-spasmed dark
still wrapped about the oar
that must have meant such promise:
hold tight tight
tight and I will save you.

Last fall, a gift my mother sent,
a burlap sack full of bulbs
she'd thinned from her own neurotic yard.
I dumped them out, palmed each one
and named them like good children
destined to make something of themselves,
who come home each year to make us proud.

Cluster of small wombs, exotic
as their names: Desert-Candle,
Tiger Flower, Star-of-Bethlehem.

Onions with a hank of hair, witch's
head or squid: Narcissus, Hyacinth.

And these like small dried fruits
all wrinkled in their skins:
Eranthus and Anemone.

But the one we could not name,
that lay twisted, small tumor
at the bottom of the sack,

nuzzled its way somehow
into November's cold layer
and, in April's punctual thaw,
pushing its head
through the indiscriminate earth,
came anyway.

Mating Season on Firethorn Pond

In a Buddhist temple in Malaysia
I saw enclosed in glass
a shell broad as a man's hand,
smooth, orbicular saucer,
and bubbled up from the pearly surface,
seven perfect baby Buddhas
small as pencil erasers,
their diapered groins
resting in lotus position

and read how long ago
a farmer scavenging the coral reefs
was drawn to the shell's silvery beauty,
how later in the temple
monks bowed each day, chanting over it
until one by one
tiny Buddhas began to rise
like blisters under scalded flesh.

Here, geese cruise in
like carloads of pubescent boys
mad for the down of necks
while along the weedy perimeter
water fizzes in microscopic sex. I drink
wine from the bottle, flop
my white feet over the edge of the pier
and watch a muskrat trail his mate,
tail of a coonskin cap,

fat cat-o-nine scudding her wrinkled way
across the pond. Three times
she bristles, rolling him
like a pine from a logging truck. I think

of monks brooding their days
over some shell, imagine
whatever god there is
prefers proliferation
the way a muskrat, rebuffed
again and again, hangs finally on,
surfing the spiny back of his love,
that sleek, tenable tail
into ecstasy.

 *Thunder*

My husband calls
from his month-long trip to California
still nursing the anger
he left me holding like a small child
in the dwindling window of the airport

and hears from my side of the continent
the crack of thunder.
And yes, yes
that is what he misses most
about South Carolina.

Not the dust rising
in red puffs above the corn.
Not the lakes of carp and catfish
turning deep
in their tentative dreams of flight.

But the way
when the land is long given up for dead
and farmers have disinherited the sky
for good this time
it breaks sudden and big as forgiveness.

They don't have that here, he says
as if he were speaking
of grits or Dixie Beer
or a woman
who would stand in a storm
holding the receiver to the sky.

Mysteries

After love
it is a game we play,
explaining the unexplainable.
Like what happens to the wax
in dripless candles.
Or why when we remember childhood
it is always summer.

And the one I think but never ask.
How day after day across five counties
you drive that old pick-up
hauling bright bins of tools,
racks of shiny utensils,
praising the virtues of your hammers and nails
as if your wares could save the world.

Tonight the mystery you give me
is how we never see
those thick slabs of tire
when they tear away from the rims of semis,
from the rims of eighteen wheelers,
the way the soul must leave the body
dying in its sleep.
But always there they are
in the fog of morning,
collapsed on the edge of the freeway
like fallen angels.

I turn to offer my explanation,
but already you are sleeping
and I can only guess
why your face still smiles:

Good love.
Because the bolts and lags
of another month
have again equalled our second mortgage.

Because all night in your dreams
heaven and earth hang level on their hinges,
their rafters held high and sturdy.

Like the reason
that inscrutable beast the camel
smiles his mysterious smile:
because in all the world
there are ninety-nine names for God
and only he knows the hundredth.

Hanging the Screens

August. Sunday. In the distance
a congregation of thunderheads
like heavy nuns enroute to mass
and because the thing I love most
is to sit in my study during a storm,
the windows up, curtains billowing
like muses above my typewriter,
my husband decides he will hang the screens
our builder never got around to.

We own no ladder, so he hauls the screens
upstairs where he lifts himself
backwards through the window,
head and shoulders out, legs in,
wrapped tight around my waist to anchor him
while he nails the silver brackets to the outside frames.

His arms are damp with sweat
and his torso trembles as he leans out
like a telephone repairman strapped to a pole,
trusting his climbing belt, his gaffs digging
into creosote, his head poking
through networks of wires and voices.

From the road a passerby might marvel
at the back of half a man emerging
from a window and inside, a woman
grasped close to the sill—
a position no missionary would take.

Or my husband's mother walking in,
as usual unannounced, would find us there,

would pale at the sight of her son
and that woman he married, entangled in lust.

He reaches for a bracket as the rain begins
and I'm thinking of Marcy Halle's tombstone
circa 1710:

> *Here lies one whose life threads cut asunder.*
> *She was struck dead by a clap of thunder.*

What better way to go than this—
clasped in my husband's thighs high above earth,
knowing how the legend will grow:
years later, tourists lining the sidewalk,
cupping hands over their children's ears, whispering
how once a man and a woman died making love
in that window, oblivious to the storm,
the charged particles converging
like flocks of yellow birds
until their bodies glowed
and lightning became their dying faces.

The Love That Ended Yesterday in Texas is the winner of the 1990 first-book competition in the TTUP Poetry Award Series. The competition was supported generously by The <u>CH</u> Foundation and the Helen Jones Foundation in honor of the sisters Christine DeVitt and Helen DeVitt Jones.